THE UNEXPLAINED

ESP

BY ADAM STONE

TORQUE™

BELLWETHER MEDIA · MINNEAPOLIS, MN

Are you ready to take it to the extreme?
Torque books thrust you into the action-packed world
of sports, vehicles, mystery, and adventure. These books
may include dirt, smoke, fire, and dangerous stunts.
WARNING: read at your own risk.

Library of Congress Cataloging-in-Publication Data

Stone, Adam.
 ESP / by Adam Stone.
     p. cm. -- (Torque: The unexplained)
  Summary: "Engaging images accompany information about ESP. The combination of high-
interest subject matter and light text is intended for students in grades 3 through 7"--Provided
by publisher.
 Includes bibliographical references and index.
 ISBN 978-1-60014-499-8 (hardcover : alk. paper)
 1. Extrasensory perception--Juvenile literature. I. Title. II. Title: E.S.P.

BF1321.S85 2010
133.8--dc22   2010008487

This edition first published in 2011 by Bellwether Media, Inc.

Printed in the United States of America, North Mankato, MN.

080110   1162

CONTENTS

CHAPTER I
A VISION OF JUPITER

In 1973, artist and author Ingo Swann claimed to have taken a voyage to Jupiter. He said that he traveled to the planet using only his mind. Swann was part of a research program paid for by the United States Central Intelligence Agency (CIA). The program was called Stargate. It studied a kind of extrasensory perception called **remote viewing**. This is the ability to view a distant location with only the mind.

Researchers monitored Swann as he took his journey. He reported seeing Jupiter's colored bands. He also said that he saw a ring around the planet. At the time, people didn't know Jupiter had a ring. It was discovered shortly after Swann's experiment. Swann also described mountains and icebergs. Scientists said those features were impossible on Jupiter. Had Swann really used remote viewing to see Jupiter, or was it all a **hoax**?

7

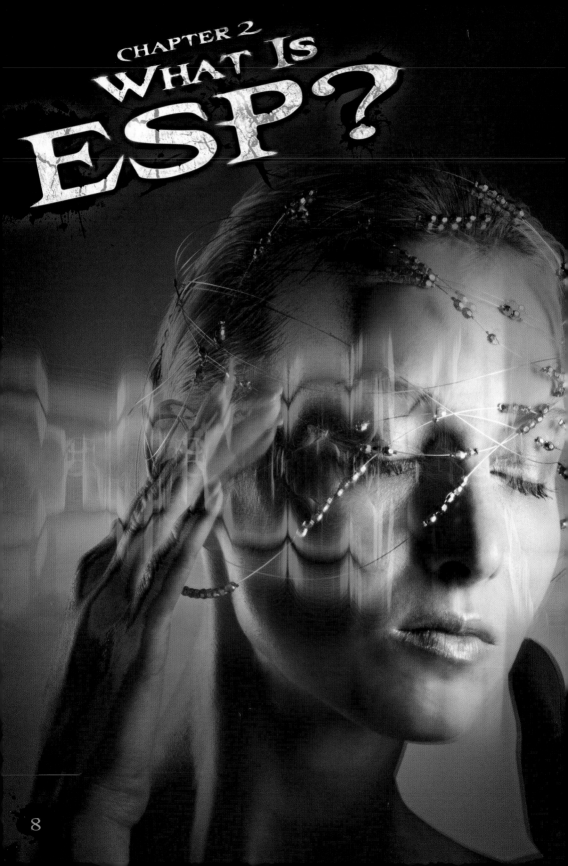

CHAPTER 2

WHAT IS ESP?

The term ESP stands for "extrasensory perception." People with ESP can see and know things without using the senses of sight, hearing, smell, taste, or touch. They claim to have extra, unexplained senses.

DÉJÀ VU

Have you ever had the feeling you are experiencing the same event a second time? This is called déjà vu. Some people think it is a form of ESP.

There are three main kinds of ESP. They are **precognition**, **clairvoyance**, and **telepathy**. Precognition is the ability to see a future event. **Psychics** are said to have this power. Clairvoyance is the ability to use the mind rather than the eyes to see a place or event. Remote viewing is a controlled type of this ability. Telepathy is the ability to send thoughts to someone else. It is also used to read someone's mind.

Uri Geller

Some people also include **psychokinesis** as a form of ESP. This is the ability to move objects with the mind. Uri Geller and others claim to use their minds to bend spoons.

Joseph Banks Rhine began researching ESP in the late 1920s. He created the term ESP, and also founded the parapsychology lab at Duke University.

Joseph Banks Rhine

HISTORY OF THE MYSTERY

Year

1500s

1898

1915

1920s

1960s

1960s

1973

1980s

1988

Event

A man named Nostradamus writes many predictions about the future, some of which seem to come true over the next several hundred years.

Author Morgan Robertson writes a story of an ocean liner named *Titan* that sinks after striking an iceberg; fourteen years later, *Titanic* suffers that exact fate.

Dr. John E. Coover conducts the first scientifically controlled experiments on psychokinesis and finds no evidence of its existence.

Joseph Banks Rhine creates the term ESP and begins his research.

Tests show that Russian psychic Roza Kuleshova can "see" colors using just her hands.

Pavel Stepanek guesses thousands of times which of two hidden cards is being held; he is correct 57 percent of the time.

As part of the CIA's Stargate experiment, Ingo Swann claims to journey to Jupiter through remote viewing.

Uri Geller amazes audiences by appearing to bend spoons with the power of his mind.

The U.S. National Research Council concludes that no scientific evidence of ESP exists.

CHAPTER 3

SEARCHING FOR ANSWERS

People have been studying ESP for decades. They use many methods. Some tests check for telepathy. In one test, a wall separates two people. One person is shown a card. The other person guesses what is on the card. In another study, researchers test for clairvoyance. They ask a subject to identify a hidden card.

J. G. Pratt (left) tests Hubert Pearce (right) for clairvoyance using Zener cards.

Zener cards

PICK A CARD

Some ESP tests use standard playing cards, but most use Zener cards. In the 1930s, Dr. Karl Zener designed five special cards for ESP research.

If ESP does exist, what is it? Is it a special gift that only a few people have? Some people say it is a power that all people have, but only some can use. Others think the ability can be unlocked with training and practice.

SIXTH SENSE

Do some people have a sixth sense? Many claim they can sense terrible events like car accidents and fires with their minds.

The human mind is complex. Tests have shown that humans use only a small fraction of their brainpower. Who knows what we might be capable of if we used it all? Would we unlock the power of ESP, or is ESP just a fantasy?

Psychic Jeane Dixon predicted that President John F. Kennedy would die in office. She also predicted that Russia would beat the United States to the moon. One prediction was right, and one was wrong. Do you think she had ESP?

HIT AND MISS

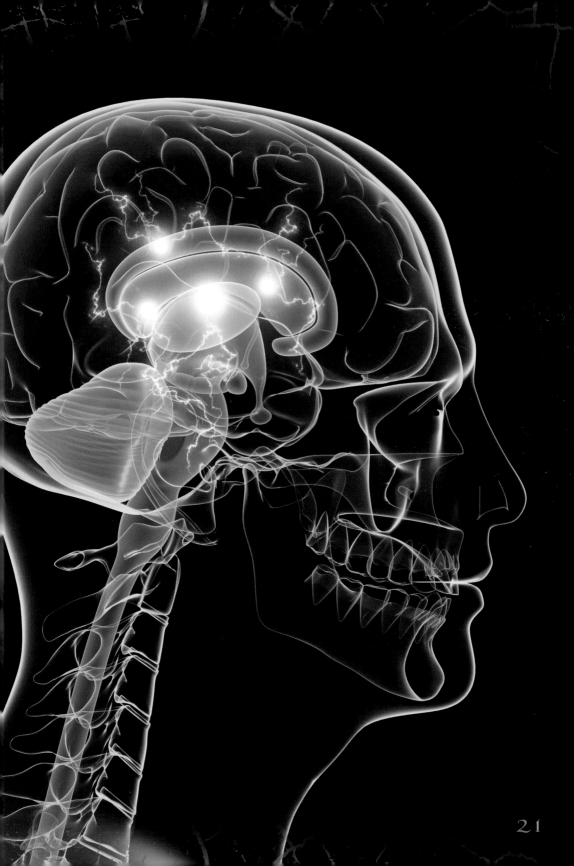

GLOSSARY

clairvoyance—the ability to use the mind to see places or events

hoax—an attempt to trick people into believing something

precognition—the ability to see or predict future events

psychics—people who use the power of precognition to predict future events

psychokinesis—the ability to use the mind to affect and move objects

remote viewing—a form of clairvoyance in which a person can travel to and view a distant place in his or her mind

telepathy—the ability to send one's thoughts to another or read the thoughts of another

TO LEARN MORE

AT THE LIBRARY

Hile, Kevin. *ESP*. Farmington Hills, Mich.: KidHaven Press, 2009.

Oxlade, Chris. *The Mystery of ESP*. Chicago, Ill.: Heinemann Library, 2008.

Tilden, Thomasine E. Lewis. *Mind Readers: Science Examines ESP*. New York, N.Y.: Franklin Watts, 2008.

ON THE WEB

Learning more about ESP is as easy as 1, 2, 3.

1. Go to www.factsurfer.com.

2. Enter "ESP" into the search box.

3. Click the "Surf" button and you will see a list of related Web sites.

With factsurfer.com, finding more information is just a click away.

INDEX

The images in this book are reproduced through the courtesy of: Jon Eppard, front cover, pp. 17 (small), 18-19; Detlev Van Ravenswaay/Photo Researchers, Inc., pp. 4-5; Mark Garlick/Photo Researchers, Inc., pp. 6-7; Yuri Arcurs, pp. 6-7; Coneyl Jay/Photo Researchers, Inc., pp. 8-9; Pete Saloutos, pp. 10-11; Ralf Juergens/Getty Images, p. 12; Bob Jordan/AP Images, p. 13; Simone Van Der Berg, pp. 14-15; Mary Evans Picture Library/Alamy, pp. 16-17; Sebastian Kaulitzki, pp. 20-21.